Table of Contents

I0476320

1. Introduction

He was a visionary, a legend and a folk hero of the 20th century who revolutionized the entertainment industry in a way that that nobody thought possible. He transformed animation into an art form and built a synergistic empire which combined television, music and theme parks. He was Walt Disney.

Following the vision of a better world he developed in his early years, he managed to create new reality meant to help people escape from the worries of everyday life. The steps he made and the actions he took transformed the world of animation and entertainment forever. Learning from ups and downs he eventually challenged the preexisting standards in art and business. He followed his motive and has proven his exceptionality to the world.

This book is designed to firstly guide you through the Walt Disney's life-changing situations and expose you to the highs and lows he encountered. Secondly it is meant to provide a deeper understanding of Disney's frame of mind and behavior that helped him to become a legend. Through his life-changing situations, we will pinpoint the morals of the stories that shaped and guided his actions which, combined with practical advices, can help you to start transforming your realities. This book, therefore, presents itself as a useful tool for bringing the knowledge and wisdom of this exceptional individual closer to you.

Finally, this book encapsulates illustrations the underlying mechanisms that propel creative thinking and behavior. It combines the knowledge learned from Walt Disney's life changing events with a multidimensional approach to explain the underlying mechanisms of creative thinking in behavior. With help of most recent findings from cognitive science and psychology it dismantles the connections between environmental influences, personal traits and creativity in the attempt to create a framework for realizing the importance of creativity on one side, and understanding how to apply its notions to increase creative output.

The knowledge accumulated within a lifetime of this great mind can therefore help you to understand your surrounding better and to take advantage of its opportunity in an effective manner that will allow your creativity to prosper and help you to overcome any obstacles in your life productively and efficiently.

2. Brief Summary of Walt Disney's life

Born on December 5, 1901 in Chicago's Hermosa community area to Irish-Canadian father and German-American mother Wald Disney was one of five children that carried out Elias's and Floras' last name into the world. The farmland in Marceline, Missouri would present the playground of young Walt for next couple of years. It was there, surrounded with nature and closest family members, where he started to draw, paint, and even sell the pictures he made to neighbors and family friends.

After four years of rustic life the family moved to Kansas City in 1911. While Walt finished the second grade at Marceline, he had to repeat the grade at the Benton Grammar School. While shocked at first, he later found the opportunity to make the best of the situation. Soon he started to spend most Saturdays at Kansas City Art Institute, improving on his drawing skills and allowing his love for art in general to grow and flourish. Still subjected to the watching eye of his father, he started working—alongside with his brother Roy—on the delivery route for The Kansas City Star, which Elias purchased soon after they moved to the new city. Working most of the days delivering papers Walt's grades suffered, but his love for drawing survived.

During the World War I Walt continue developing his drawing skills. The war theme was a perfect choice for this young patriot and soon he started to publish his patriotic cartoon in the high school newspaper. After his family moved yet again, this time to Chicago in 1917 when his father became a shareholder of a local factory, he was enrolled to McKinley High school. While perfecting his skills at the Chicago Academy of Fine Arts, the school was happy to give him the opportunity to display his passionate support for the troops in his own unique way. Helpful suggestions like "Eat less so there could be more food for soldiers overseas!" became a part of his routine.

Following his elder brother Roy, who joined the Navy, as well as Herbert and Ray who served in the army, Walt dropped out of high school with a hope to join the armed forces. The fact that he was only 16 at the time contributed to the rejection. However, he was able to find an alternative. One of his early artistic endeavors, where he changed the birth date on his passport, enabled him to join the Red Cross Ambulance Corps, which allowed 17 year-olds to join their operation.

After his time in France ended, Disney moved to Kansas City in 1919. His endeavors in the field of art made him rethink his future. The usual work routine just wasn't his cup of tea and he decided to pursue an artistic career. Political caricatures and comic books were his first attempt in getting an employment;

however nobody wanted to hire him. By then he has already proven that he didn't care much about obstacles that might come his way. Together with his brother Roy he then started to create advertisements for newspapers and magazines at the local art studio. Being only 18 years of age he made his first solid steps into the business of animation.

It was in May 1922 when Walt prepared the paperwork to establish the Laugh-O-Gram Studio. His goal at this point was to create short animated movies for movie theaters and alike. The recruitment of his previous co-worker Fred Hartman followed and soon the first cartoons from the Laugh-O-Gram series were presented to the public. Their popularity grew and money started to pile.

However, the profits quickly dropped and after a short while they were simply insufficient to cover the operation costs of the studio and the paychecks for the employees. The lack of founds quickly started to sink the Studio deeper and deeper into debt.

In their final attempt the studio started to focus on Alice Comedies, a series of animated cartoons which firstly presented to the public the live action little girl Alice placed, together with her cat, in an animated environment.

While widely accepted as a cute and funny, the success of these 10-minute cartoons simply didn't reach the much needed level that the studio was aiming for. The financial situation continued to worsen and it didn't take long until Walt Disney went bankrupt.

Not yet twenty-two, with his suitcase in one hand and an unfinished print of the Alice Comedies in the other, the impoverished Disney left Kansas City and moved to Hollywood. Two months after his arrival in October 1923 he and his brother Roy, who was already living in California, set up a shop in their uncle's garage. With barely having enough money between them for paying rent yet alone to start a new business, the venture seemed too daring. Tenacious as they were they found a place they could afford, a small room at the back of a real estate office. Roy took control of the camera, Walt did the animation and two girls hired to ink and paint the celluloids helped them to realize their ideas. The Disney Bros. Studio was born.

However the beginnings were rough and the brothers were in a search for assistance in reaching the public. Margaret Winkler, a distributer from New York, couldn't hide her enthusiasm and live-action animation based upon Alice's Wonderland was made. The first of the new Allice series was delivered at the end of the year, and the studio earned the first paycheck. While the amount wouldn't even cover the average rent in today's time, it was enough for keeping Alice alive for years.

Although the combination of financial boost and Walt's enthusiasm enabled him to swing to the top of

Hollywood industry in no time, he showed no interest for Hollywood's popularity contest. He rather focused on his private life. His conversational abilities and charm had an obvious effect on Lillian Bounds, one of Walt's first employees. In July 1925 they got married and later, after their first attempt at pregnancy ended in miscarriage, they would be blessed with the birth of Diane Marie Disney in 1933. Three years later the couple decided to adopt another girl and Sharon Mae Disney joined the family.

By 1927 the "Alice idea" had exhausted itself and the series had lost popularity. It was time to move on. In 1926 Disney's studio received an order for another series of animation. Walt's numerous ideas and vivid imagination needed some taming and the input of his oldest friend Ub Iwerks was needed. The collaboration between them gave birth to the Oswald the Lucky Rabbit, an anthropomorphic creature, which instantly became highly popular figure in American culture.

Oswald the Lucky Rabbit became widely recognized. This unique furry character, which represented a new standard in cartoon animation, starred in more than 190 films. Growing demand called for the increase of the production costs and the contract signed in New York soon didn't cover the expenses anymore. As the growing success and the recognition of the series resulted in high merchandise performance, Disney well-versed in the trade soon realized that increasing his share of the pie could boost the studio's financial performance. The 20% cut on the films he was receiving didn't seem a reasonable amount anymore and in February 1928 he left California to negotiate the higher fee for producing the series.

Endowed with optimism and with a clear vision of the future of the series he arrived to New York. Not only that his request was denied, but Charles Mintz, the head of the Universal Pictures, had even more shocking news prepared for him. Walt was told that the employment agreements with all of his crew were already negotiated, which meant that each and every creator of the beloved series was now working for Mintz's company directly. Walt was no longer an essential component of the process and the Oswald series could be created without him. His creation and all his staff were stolen right out from under him.

Walt needed to create. He needed something to replace the lost star of his cartoons, and inspired by his pet mouse (which he had adopted while working in Kansas City) he started to develop a new character. Ub Iwerks, a loyal friend who, unlike the others, decided to stay with Disney, was the artistic tool who helped to enliven this idea and Mickey Mouse was soon born.

With Walt giving him his soul (and until 1947 also his voice) he first appeared in a silent cartoon. The public indifference and the inability to find an adequate distributer for the film could again set the partners back financially. However, their opportunity came with the introduction of the sound-synchronization techniques to the cartoon animation and Mickey starring in Steamboat Willie became an immediate success. The public found his sound enriched creation appealing more than ever and called for more. Silly Symphonies soon followed the footsteps of the world's most beloved mouse.

Being a devotee of new technologies and techniques of animation he soon adopted the new medium of Technicolor. When Herbert Kalmus, a scientist and engineer who played a key role in developing color motion picture, approached him with the idea, Disney already had his Flowers and Trees, a Silly Symphony cartoon, in production. This however didn't stop him from jumping on the idea. He trashed the partially completed film and restarted the process. His vision, while seen by others as madness, proved to be a success: the movie was a sensation and it draw the attention from public as well as the other film studios. The world was at the doorstep of a new era of animation.

In 1934, when the United States and the rest of the world were hindered by the strong grip of the Great Depression, Walt decided that the world was ready for the first full-length animation feature. No wonder that the film industry marked his project as "Disney's Folly". The venture seemed unreasonable and would surely lead to downfall of Disney's studios.

However, Disney—stubborn as always—would not be distracted by the fuss and continue experimenting with the realistic human animation, the development of the distinctive character animation and using special effects, including multiplane cameras technique that he grew fond of when producing The Old Mill, short feature of Silly Symphonies. All of this innovative techniques and efforts were focused in producing the Snow White and the Seven Dwarfs, the feature that would change the quality standards of cartons on one side and the expectation of the public on the other.

After initial issues and financial challenges, the movie was released in 1937 with huge success. Disney reached a new high in his glory and wealth and was able to open a new campus for the Walt Disney Studios two years later. Additional features, including Fantasia, Bambi, Peter Pan and Pinocchio soon followed. While some of them did not reach the same public acceptance as their forerunner, they shifted the industry to the next level and provided Disney with a springboard that would elevate him to the top of the list of most influential people in the world.

In 1941, shortly after Disney's Dumbo was released, the U.S. entered the World War II. Well-familiar with the field of war animation, Disney was soon approached by the government officials. Walt—patriot, true American, businessman and animation innovator, didn't hesitate in his decision and it wasn't long until Disney studios' facilities were contracted by the U.S. army.

Disney's role as a public morale builder reflected in his involvement in basically every branch of the U.S. military and government. His studios provided instructional videos for sailors and soldiers. More than 90% of Disney's employees devoted their knowledge and experience to propaganda film and through the means of animated graphics helped the U.S, government in the mobilization of civilians and servicemen.

When the war was over, the ever restless Disney started to look around in search for other possibilities the world might have for him. When visiting California's Children's Fairyland in Oakland he finally understood what was left to be done. Soon after, on a business trip to Chicago in the late 1940s he drew sketches of his vision of the most perfect amusement park. The idea included his employees spending time with children in an opened space designed to provide fun and relaxation for the whole family. Brainstorming soon materialized the concept that formed a cornerstone for Disney's next great business venture: Disneyland.

In the last years of his life, he interested himself in providing the public with a space for enabling creativity. Few years before his death on December 15, 1966 he contributed to establishment of California

Institute of the Arts, which merged the L.A. Conservatory of Music and Chouinard Art Institute.

3. Creativity Lessons from Walt Disney

Whether we are trying to express our feelings and moods or find a new way to solve a problem at work we are driven by a force that propels our thinking capabilities and gives us the chance to think outside the box. Creativity has been pegged to conductive environments, personality traits, serendipity, and even spiritual muses. Recent findings from the field of cognitive science imply that creative thinking is driven by factors, which could be roughly categorized in three classes: from **above**, **within**, and **without**:

Inspiration from creative thinking and behavior from **within** could be understood as a set of unconsciously produced ideas and beliefs. In other words, it derives from you.

Factors from **above** can be regarded as triggers—the moments of revelations—which are directed toward the application of existing knowledge into work of art or some other concrete factors. Because of their inherent nature it is impossible to influence on those factors: they simply occur when they do.

Creativity factors from **without** refer to environmental influences that can trigger an innovative or artistic behavior. These factors can include nature as well as people. To allow them to affect you, keeping an open mind is essential; otherwise important environmental cues could be missed and overlooked. Objects or people are capable of evoking creative thinking and behavior only in the case you can put aside your tendency to perceive them narrowly.

As the first two categories are in their essence of personal origins, we will focus on environmental factors that can stimulate your creativity. Walt Disney will serve as a subject of creative impetus and will allow us to not only to learn from his decisions but to transform them into guidelines for enhancing creative behavior. By applying these lessons to your situation, you will be able to overcome your creative block and rethink your problem solving abilities.

3.1 Make Your Own Realities

"I suppose my formula might be: dream, diversify and never miss an angle."

~Walt Disney

We are defined by our social and natural environment; and our role in it greatly depends on its characteristics and features. Like a bird, who takes all the opportunities that the opens sky has to offer and transforms them into advantages, so are we prone to make the best out of the situations we were born in. Nevertheless, a bird's advantages derives from having access to the sky, and locking it in a cage would limit its potential and, together with its environment, change the nature of his role.

The same goes for us; being trapped in an unfertile environment, despite of our immense desire to learn, grow, and develop can quickly clip our wing and mold us to fit into the model. However, there is a unique capability which birds were not blessed with: humans have the ability to create the escape from inconveniences of our everyday life by imagining our possibilities and acting towards our desires. Let's see how this works in the real-life example:

Walt Disney's childhood was far from picturesque. Elias, Walt's father, was a man of discipline an deeds. He was a harsh authoritarian who did not think twice when it came to strict parenting. They say that though love is one of the best parenting styles, the "disciplinary" beating that Walt and his brother Roy were daily subjected to, served as a counter effect.

Rather than focusing his energy and attention to learning in school he found an escape from his father rigid attitude in imagination. With the help of a simple pen and some ink he distanced himself from the cruel and unfair reality and put his ever evolving imagination into action. He created his own fantasy world, his heaven on earth, his utopia where the people were always happy, the sun was always shining and everything there was meant to perfect the whole. What was even more important is the fact that this allowed him to be in perfect control of what was going on in this world of his. Nobody controlled him, no one oppressed him. His world was what he was;

uninhibited and positive. He made his own reality that helped him to escape the worries of everyday life and focus on his creativity impulses.

When you find yourself restrained by difficult circumstances in your life, just remember that:

1) Life is heterogeneous and complex

It sometimes seems that we are stuck in our progress while everything else is passing by with the speed of life. This devastating feeling (and this is a fact that you have to realize) presents only one short moment in your lifetime. If you look at it from perspective you will see that diversity of thing you have done in your life is immense: you spend a portion of your time here on earth in school; another portion to master a skill that you need to be superb in your job; and a part of it to enjoy time with the love of your life. It could be said that you already had more than one life—each of those periods could be regarded as an entity. Now imagine how many things you still could do in the future. They say that it takes about 7 years to master something. In the case you live to be 88, after age 11, you will have 11 opportunities to be great at something.

2) Your inner child stays with you forever

When we grow up and we become limited in our time by our responsibilities and duties, it is difficult to envision that we are all still basically children. Time had passed since we monkeyed around carelessly, inventing new games and making up our own rules to live by. Children are children because they don't know yet how they should behave. They simply let their imagination go its course and in attempt to enjoy themselves, they blindly follow it. By stepping away from constraints of everyday life for an hour or two a week, you could do the same. Act childish for a change and be irrational for a while. When everything goes ok, and when you will see that you can still function within the norms of society later on, you will see that it is not impossible or even prohibited to make a better world for yourself.

3) Affective visualization can guide through life choices

When you will start to realize the possibilities of imagining your possible realities and start to enjoy them, you will open the door to a completely new world of opportunities. By applying emotions to your day-dreams and fantasies you will transform them into something you want to reach. You will make goals out of them and soon your imaginary realities will become real.

3.2 Acknowledge and Prepare for Obstacles

"All the adversity I've had in my life, all my troubles and obstacles have strengthened me... You may not realize when it happens, but a kick in the teeth may be the best thing in the world for you."

~Walt Disney

Obstacles exist and will continue in the future and there is nothing we can do about it. Whenever we have a desire we want to appease, there is a great chance that something or someone will be there (intentionally or not) to make our journey just a bit more difficult.

Walt Disney was far from exceptional in this regard. Soon in his life he realized that some things are not meant to be easy and that the only thing he can do about it is to prepare himself for potential issues and always stay one step ahead of them. Especially clearly he demonstrated this attitude when he, still under aged, tried (and succeed) to join the U.S army in their actions oversees. Instead of giving up after the first rejection, he went back home and prepared for the next trial. By incorporating his artistic skills he managed to persuade the officials who allowed him to join the Army and go overseas to France when he was not yet 17.

Disney learned his lesson based on the value of preparation for obstacles which can stand on the way of reaching desired goals, and provided you with the option to do the same. Don't pretend that obstacles are just an illusion which will disappear when you reach it. Some bridges are not meant to be crossed when you come to them they could be a call for preparation, especially the ones with a huge hole in the middle.

From this perspective obstacles of all changes and sizes can hinder you on your path towards your goals; however they can be quite beneficial also. They will call for an active effort for resolving them, and the preparatory phase can have a positive influence on the outcome of your actions.

1) Concurring the status-quo bias

Overcoming obstacles requires effort and mental strength, and sometimes they can be strong enough to decide not to follow your dreams. This can eventually transform into behavioral and thought patterns which could lead to habit-creation and become deeply entrenched over time. As a result you will tend to stay in your comfort zone and stick with things you are most familiar with.

With anticipating potential obstacles you will start to break that pattern. Newly formed mental patterns will start to transform into new behavioral traits. This, at first demanding task will soon become a part of your attitudes towards challenges. The hindrances will eventually constitute as your short-term goals which you will subconsciously start to incorporate into your plans of actions.

2) Overcoming the loss-aversion bias

Research in psychology and behavioral economics have shown that losing something have a greater negative impact on our mood wining the exact equivalent amount would have a positive one. In many cases this reason is enough to avert you from going for something you really like. However, realizing the existence of this effect can provide an opportunity to overcome it with pure willpower. When you know and understand that there is something else, something that could potentially change your life, waiting behind the obstacle, there are no more reasonable grounds for this bias to be effective. But there is still an emotional component to it.

Of course there is a chance that you won't succeed. However this doesn't mean that you will never succeed. Maybe it just means that you weren't ready at the moment, and the simple realization of this will help you in the future. Use this as a chance to encourage your emotional growth and prepare for potential obstacles by focusing on your emotional stability. As seen from the case of Walt Disney, it can also help you in your future ventures.

3.3 Failure is Merely a Mental Construct: Wire Yourself for Success

"It's kind of fun to do the impossible."

~Walt Disney

The story of Laugh-O-Gram studio is a clear example that success and failure begins in our thought. How we act upon that will guide us in our actions in the future.

Disney clearly had an understanding of that as he took the lesson he learned from the bankruptcy of his studio and rather focused on the future. Instead of grasping on the past occurrences he devoted himself to work and with understanding that a possibility of a failure which is beyond his reach could always exist. This shaped his approach and turned him into the legend he still is today.

Memory can play a great role in shaping the behavioral attitudes towards a challenge. Learning from mistakes and not letting them to bring you down or disable you completely is an effort-intensive skill. Emotions are usually the driving force behind irrational action. Bad experience in the past can result in a tendency to avoid similar situation in a future, although there might be no apparent connection between them. The memory, especially emotional part of it, plays an important part in this process and affectively editing it can remove bed feelings associated with particular memories and replace them with positives one.

Think of your memory as a video and memory recall as a video editing process. When you are involved in activity you record the signals that come from the environment through the process of forming new neural connections. Each of the stimuli that you perceive will influence this process which will result in creation of complex neural network. This enables you to store intricate information about that particular activity, including emotions and feelings.

Recalling your memory activates these connections again and allows you to have the mental representation of the activity in question; you remember the colors, the smells, the conversations and, of course, how you felt at the time. Because these neural connections are active when you attend a similar activity at a later time (which actually allows you to learn), the emotions are also transferred. When you felt good in the activity in the past, you won't have any trouble to perform in the present or future event, however when the emotion connected to the experience is far on the negative side, the transfer could meant that you will try to avoid the action-and the feeling associated- completely.

As the video can be edited in order to meet our aesthetic demand so can the memory. There is a possibility to intentionally edit bad memories to remove the bad feelings and emotions associated with bad memories:

1) Editing bad memories

You can edit your bed memories so they don't hold you back with the help of few simple exercises. Bring your memory into your mind, and then imagine it getting smaller and dimmer. Transform the picture, get rid of the colors and try to make it as blurry as possible. Next add details that will scramble the memory. Include details that would unlikely be true (strange setting, celebrities that weren't actually there and so on). Finally, involve emotions that that coincide with the new emotion. Make them vivid and powerful to ensure that they will stick. Try to repeat the exercise 5 to 10 times.

2) Editing good memories

You can increase the power of good memories that will propel you forward by applying the same technique. Involve as much positives emotions and as many vivid and perceivable sound, visual or tactile stimuli. Again, perform the exercise 5 to 10 times.

The fact that we can forget quite a bit and that we are not always in touch with the idea that our memories can sometimes be misleading is fairly well known. Usually this presents a problem, especially in the case of witness testimony in the court of law. The positive side of this is that it is possible to use this knowledge and findings from psychology to reverse-engineer our own memories in order not to be completely defined by our actions from the past. Failure in this regard becomes only a mental construct that we can avoid by rewiring ourselves for success.

3.4 Keep Your Drive Alive

"A person should set his goals as early as he can and devote all his energy and talent to getting there."

~Walt Disney

When Disney wasn't even 22 years of age, he gathered his belongings and headed to California to start over. With a clear vision in his mind and full of energy, he did not look back at his failed attempt to start his business in Kansas City but rather regrouped his thoughts and focus his attention on the future. Keeping the drive alive was soon proven to be the attitude that would result in repeated success.

One of the most important factors of keeping your drive alive is the motivation. Staying motivated is easy when things are going according to plan, however being motivated in spite of potential washout is a completely different story.

Motivational force consists of many factors that can direct the process in which one might selects one behavioral option over another; action over inaction, or fight over flight. The combination of expectancy, valence, and instrumentality can make a difference when talking about maintaining a certain level of motivation.

1) Expectancy

Expectancy is a factor that represents the belief that your effort is an outcome of a need to reach the desired goals. In other words, it is the desire to achieve something that is propelling your actions. The goal itself represents enough reward for you to actually start working your way to reach it.

There are three factors that can (and will) influence your expectancy perception:

i. **Self-efficacy:** Your perception of your ability to perform. High self-efficacy means high expectancy.

ii. **Goal difficulty**: Goals that are set too high lead to low expectancy. On the other hand, goals that are set too low can have the same effect.

iii. **Control:** The level of your perceived control over your performance. When you experience complete control of your actions, the expectancy level is optimized.

2) Valence

The notion of valence includes the value that you set for the action of reaching for the desired goal. Reaching a goal means a reward in itself, but your personal level of pleasure coming from the behavior can greatly influence your motivation level.

When the valence is highest, the goal is highly anticipated and potential for active behavior is increased. In the other hand, when the valence is low, there is not enough force of attraction coming from the goal to initiate the action. The third option calls for an indifferent attitude towards the goal.

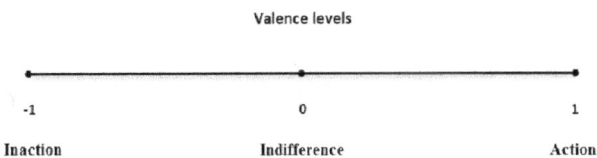

Valence levels

3) Instrumentality

The notion of instrumentality refers to the additional instruments and tool that might increase the level of satisfaction of reaching the particular goal. The reward system, as it can also be called, could comprise of intrinsic or extrinsic rewards as well as monetary or non-monetary ones. In the case the reward is similar for all the activities you need to perform, the instrumentality is low. When you reward different actions differently, and therefore use variety of tools, you increase the instrumentality and can positively influence the level of motivation.

3.5 Overcome Emotional Attachments

"Why worry? If you've done the very best you can, worrying won't make it any better."

~Walt Disney

In order to achieve great thing in live or simply maintain the ability to prepare for the future, one has to disregard the past and stay focused on the present. The importance of this frame of mind was clearly demonstrated by Disney, when he didn't allow the negative situation in the case of Oswald the Lucky Rabbit, to change his goal-oriented attitude. Despite being betrayed by his distributer and most of his employees, he kept his cool and rechanneled his energy to the next project, which would, as we now know, made a revolution in the animation industry.

Bearing in mind the actions of others when deciding for the future is not a negative thing by itself. However, it can become problematic, when clinging to other people's opinions and emotions provoked by their actions obstruct our present comfort.

When feeling negative emotions your ratio and decision-making ability are affected. Therefore it is important and much desired to let go them as soon as possible. This is especially true when the inability to let go presents an obstacle for your future well-being.

The emotional attachment theory classifies different types of emotional attachment. While not all of them are *de facto* bad it is essential to recognize them in order to make attempt to break the undesired connections.

1) Secure attachment

Securely attached adults tend to be more satisfied with their relationships with others. They offer support when their mate feels distressed and are prepared to comfort him/her when they themselves feel troubled. Their relationships tend to be honest, open and equal.

This kind of attitude reflects also on their ability to accept emotional cues from the environment. Their ability to reason with the emotions allows them to understand that there are some aspects of life that they simply can't control. In this manner it is easier for them to understand that sometimes, to feel secure, searching for a new setting is a must.

2) Anxious preoccupied attachment

People with an anxious attachment are likely to be desperate to form a fantasy bond instead of feeling genuine emotions to their partner. Because of that they often feel emotional hunger. They are constantly searching for emotional completion. In addition, their actions can be ambiguous; although they are seeking a sense of safety and security by clinging to positive emotions and the situations that allow them to experience them, they can take actions that can by themselves overwhelm the chance of such a situation.

Anxious attachment also addresses the way of approaching negative emotions caused by others. Instead of letting go of them and focusing on the present, anxiously attached individuals tend to form their present actions based on the feelings derived from their surrounding in the recent past.

3) Dismissive avoidance attachment

People with a dismissive avoidant attachment have the tendency to emotionally distance themselves from their partner. They may seek isolation and feel pseudo-independent by taking on the role of parenting themselves. They appear focused on themselves and their present comfort.

While being dismissively attached can agitate potential problems in connecting to people, it is possible for these individuals to let go of their past negative emotions easily and focus on their well-being in the present. However, this means that much of the attention is oriented towards "now" which doesn't allow much room for planning for the future.

Emotional attachment is a complex phenomenon, and the described examples are merely archetypes. In reality nothing is so straight-forward breaking emotional attachment may call for performing a thorough personal analysis in order to understand its underlying mechanisms. Whatever they might be, focus your energy on the present and try to let go of the past.

3.6 Blaze the Trail

"Around here, however, we don't look backwards for

very long. We keep moving forward, opening up new doors and doing new things, because we're curious...and curiosity keeps leading us down new paths."

~Walt Disney

Walt Disney proved himself as pioneer on the field of animation, an innovator in business and as a creator with immensely developed sense for new ideas and approaches. His desire to push the envelope, clearly seen in his ventures with Mickey Mouse, has placed him on the throne of animation industry, from where he dictated the development of new norms of the entertainment as a whole in the future. Using technology never before used in animation he managed to established prevalence over his competitors. Pat Sullivan—one of Disney's biggest rivals—with his Felix the Cat was one of the first to be eclipsed by the new star of the entertainment business. Sullivan, although well-seasoned cartoonist and pioneer animator, was actually forced to close his studio in 1932 and had to give up his supremacy to the new alpha-male of animation.

If there is one lesson to be learned from his action it has to be this one: Always push the limits of existing standards and go the extra mile to achieve great things. Pushing the envelope involves creative and innovative behavior. Creativity usually occurs in the interaction between a person's thoughts and his/her sociocultural context. In this regard it is more than a

CREATIVITY LESSONS from WALT DISNEY

systemic rather than an individual phenomenon, as it derives from the culturally promoted norms and the possibilities of the social niche the person is coming from. On the other hand, innovation requires adoption of new ideas, their implementation and diffusion. As such it is an action-driven behavior which usually results in something concrete and tangible. Creativity is the first step to innovation which can therefore be seen as the successful implementation of novel and creative ideas.

Regardless of their efforts, people can seek for novelties for a whole life-time but may never come to find something brand-new. People can and do engage in productive activity but only seldom create a new product. Crucial differences appear to exist between producing and producing something novel. Understanding this difference can be tricky, but a **Novelty generation model** can help to clarify them.

The model introduces the process of novelty-seeking as the first component of the process of **novelty generation**. After the initial steps have been done, the second phase consists of **novelty-finding** and **production of the novelty**. The process of **presenting** an innovative product **to the public** hereon falls into the final phase of the innovative cycle.

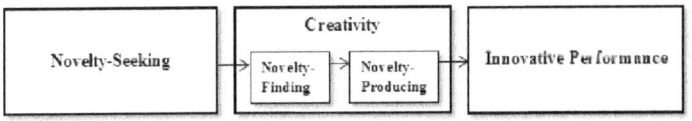

To be successful in innovative production you will firstly have to discover where there is still room for improvement. This most crucial process can take a lot of time as a lot of research is required. When you notice an opening you can start the brainstorming process about the novelty you would like to create. Production phase might not bring the desired results and a possibility of being stuck somewhere in between those two processes is relatively high. When you finally have your product it is time to get noticed and find an adequate application for it.

3.7 Balance Your Relationships: They Make You Who You Are

"A man should never neglect his family for business."

~Walt Disney

During our lifetimes we are involved in numerous and heterogeneous relationships; from platonic to intimate, from personal to business ones. They are who we are and we are what they make us to be. Ability to maintain balanced relationships is therefore crucial for a balanced self and the aptness to balance between different relationships can provide us with the opportunity to diversify our nature and grow personally.

The necessity of balancing relationships can be clearly noted in Disney's ability to combine his personal life with his business relations. While he was well known for his stoic public appearance, he was however discrepant it may be, notorious for his explosive temperament. At home, on the other side, he was a completely different person. In one of the interviews, Diane Disney, the apple of her father's eye once stated:

> Daddy never missed a father's function no matter how I discounted it. I'd say, "Oh Daddy, you don't deed to come. It's just some stupid thing." But he'd always be there, on time.

Involvement in the inexorable circumstances that shaped Disney's destiny were obviously forgotten when the situation involved his family members. The same became apparent later, when his friends marked him as a loving character, who always stayed interested in the matters of others, and was always there for his family and friends.

The ability to transform from a loving father and caring father to a vicious entrepreneur with a clear vision of success enabled him to strive in all aspects of his life. Applying emotional aspects of relationship management nurtured by his family to his business relations on one side, and being able to stay devoted to time management, a skill needed to stay organized in business, in order to be there for his family when they needed him the most.

People tend to relate to one another in one of three ways: independently, dependently and interdependently:

1) Independent relationships

In this arrangement the people involved seem unconnected and get involved in a cooperative behavior only when the situation calls for it. Emotional gap seem to exist between them, however the lack of genuine emotions is not necessary present. Independent relationships are merely a configuration which allows people involved to stay emotionally independent yet enables them to grow personally and spiritually together, when it is necessary.

2) Dependent relationships

In these relationships one person sets aside his/her personal well-being and devotes his/her energy to maintain the relationship. This gesture implies that the person who is codependent in the relationship can have troubles surviving without the other person.

3) Interdependent relationships

These relationships involve emotional intimacy but don't call for a compromise or sacrifice on one's values and ideals. This arrangement is about cooperation and cooperation. Each person is self-reliant and at the same time responsible for the other.

Knowing how personal relations can be helpful in finding the perfect balance between taking care of your needs and connecting to somebody on a deep level at the same time. However, this understanding does not help with balancing the personal relationships with professional ones. This process sometimes appears as incomprehensible and deciding about where to set priorities a tedious task. By applying your situation to the following management matrix, you could define the personal priorities and barriers you might face.

	Urgent	Not urgent
	manage	*focus*
Important	• Crisis • Medical emergencies • Pressing problems • Deadline-driven projects • Last-minute preparations for scheduled activities	• Preparation/planning • Prevention • Values clarification • Exercise • Recreation/relaxation • Relationship building/bonding
	Section of necessity	Section of personal leadership
	avoid	*avoid*
Unimportant	• Interruptions • Too many "pressing" matters • Too many popular activities • Multitasking	• Busy schedule • Time wasters • Escape activities • Procrastination
	Section of deception	Section of waste

Coordinating between what is important and what is not, what needs to be managed, which activities should be avoided and which are necessary in order to reach a balance in everyday life. The management matrix can from this point of view be applied to private and professional aspects of it.

3.8 Understand Your Unique Role

"Somehow I can't believe there are many heights that can't be scaled by a man who knows the secret of making dreams come true. This special secret can be summarized in four C's. They are curiosity, confidence, courage, and constancy, and the greatest of these is confidence."

~Walt Disney

While validation encompasses expressing understanding and acceptance of another person's internal experience, whatever that might be, self-validation is aimed towards accepting our own internal thoughts and feelings. Its importance becomes significant when we are trying to find our placement in the world.

Disney new exactly what it means to listen to your desire and to act upon them even when everyone else expresses doubt about your intentions. If he didn't, the Golden age of animation might never happen.

In 1934, when the United States and the rest of the world were hindered by the strong grip of the Great Depression, Walt decided that the world was ready for the first full-length animation feature. All of his innovative approaches and efforts were focused in producing the Snow White and the Seven Dwarfs, the feature that would change the quality standards of cartoons on one side and the expectations of the public on the other. Others that followed, including Fantasia, Bambi, Peter Pan and Pinocchio shifted the industry to the next level and provided Disney with a springboard that would elevate him to the top of the list of most influential people of the world.

Self-validation, however, doesn't mean that you believe that your thoughts or feelings are justified just because they are yours. The notion applies to the process of validating and accepting your true self, which will help you to accept and better understand your internal mental processes, which can lead to stronger identity and better skills at managing intense emotions. In other words, self-validation can help you find wisdom and the strength to control you emotionally-derived actions.

Another important aspect of understanding your unique role and true value is confidence. Disney showed in his daring ventures that he wasn't shy of it. It helped him to remain strong when others would become week and to remain faithful to his mission.

Self-confidence could be understood as the difference between the person you think you are and the person you would like to be. When the gap between those two *selves* is big, the confidence level tends to be low. Self-image, which combines the negative and imagined self, plays a crucial role here, and in order to boost confidence level, this notion has to be addressed appropriately.

1) Negative self

Negative self represents a person you believe you are. It is usually an inaccurately negative view of yourself. While it contains many aspects that you don't like about yourself, it presents itself as something that needs to be hidden from the rest or at least be ashamed of.

2) Imagined self

Imagined self derives from over-compensating for the negative image of yourself. Because you tend to dislike particular aspect of your personality or behavior you tend to create another view of yourself in your mind. The imagined self is therefore a representation of you meant for everyone else and is, as such, an unrealistic extreme.

Not living up to your expectations in the combination with extremely negative view on your real self can lower you self-confidence level; inability to reach the expectancy level could reveal all the flaws and weaknesses to the rest of the world. This kind of thinking can result in fear and prevent you from getting in touch with your true potential.

The solution lies in bringing these two views closer together. One option is to start believing that you are actually like your imagined self, and starting to act accordingly. Positive psychology has revealed that positive attitudes can have outstanding effects on behavioral traits so this might as well work.

3.9 Know How to Accommodate

"The way to get started is to quit talking and begin doing."

~Walt Disney

Sometimes your predicament calls for its acceptance and the subsequent alteration of norms and behaviors. Even Disney had to redesign his production capabilities in order to help his country in war time. However he adapted to the new setting and made the best out of it. His actions in that time only helped him to alleviate him in the eyes of public which helped him to become a national idol after the war.

Accommodation refers to exactly that. It is the part of the adaptation process, which involves altering existing schemas and ideas as a result of new experiences coming from a different situation. It also calls for creation of new schemas that can help to adapt to the changes quicker and easily.

Some situations require radical transformation of ideals and norms, as well as an upgrade of the ability for applying the pre-existing knowledge. When new information that conflicts with existing schemas appear, it is crucial to accommodate this new learning in order to assure that your thoughts and attitudes conforms to what is happening in the real world.

However, accommodation should be always accompanied by assimilation. There must always be enough accommodation to adapt to the new situations and enough assimilation to do it quickly and efficiently.

In other words, there should be a state of equilibrium established between these processes. One part of it should consist of understanding the importance of changing the behavioral and thinking patterns that can help you to achieve optimal results, and the other one from the ability to do it as fast as possible when the situation demands. Similar to Disney's case where he accepted the new and unexpected state of war and kept his production going by reorganizing his facilities.

3.10 Strive to Make a Difference

*"The greatest moments in life are not concerned with
selfish achievements but rather with the things we do
for people we love and esteem."*

~Walt Disney

Social and cultural niches provide us with everything
we need to become who we are. We are born into it,
and without drastic actions we cannot escape from it.
We adopt its values and ideals and it provides a
structure that makes us who we are.

Our environment comprises of individuals who are
responsible for its development and growth. Personal
contributions of everyone included are combined into
the common strive for progress. This places everyone
in the position of important donor of vision and ideas.

Disney demonstrated his understanding of his role in
the society not only with providing with means of
entertainment, but even more when he started to
direct his resources into designing a place for
development of future beautiful minds.

His ideas materialized when the Disney Corporation
purchased a large chunk of land in the center of
Florida State and started planning of a new, upgraded
Disney world, which would include a hotel vacation
center, newly designed theme park and his
experimental community of tomorrow. Walt's growing
enthusiasm about the public interest become even
more present with the establishment of the California

Institute of the Arts in 1961, just five years prior to his death in 1966.

He gave something back to the community, not because he felt obligated to do so, but rather because of his unselfish concern for other people. His behavior involved doing things simply out of a desire to help and originated from feeling of obligation, duty or loyalty. It originated in altruistic impulses.

Reasons for altruistic behavior are numerous and can be observed from different perspectives. While they tend to focus on different aspects of our existence, examining them soon reveals that we are made for helping others.

1) Biological reasons

Researches have shown that we tend to be more altruistic towards those who are related to us. This might be so because helping them also increases the odds that our blood relations will survive and transmit their genes to future generations.

2) Neurological reasons

Altruistic behavior also activates reward centers in the brain. When we are engaged in an altruistic act, the brain pleasure points, which are usually activated by the things we enjoy, are involved in the process. This means that we actually enjoy helping others in the same way we enjoy eating chocolate or having sex.

3) Social reasons

Society's norms, expectations, and rules also influence whether or not people engage in altruistic act. One of those is the norm of reciprocity. It is a social expectation in which we feel obligated to help other if they have already done something similar for us in the past.

4) Cognitive reasons

Although altruism usually involves an act without the anticipation of reward, the cognitive incentives may still exist. It is possible that we help others to relieve our own distress. In this regard being kind to others upholds our view of ourselves as empathetic and kind people.

The empathy itself could be a major factor in altruistic behavior. Researches have shown that we are more likely to engage in altruistic act when we feel empathy for the person who is in distress. Whether this helps us to feel better about ourselves, or it is purely an internal mechanism that forces us to help each other in order to survive as a community is not clear. What is clear though is that seeing another person in trouble causes us to feel upset and uncomfortable, which is in most cases good enough reason to help the person in trouble.

Whatever your reasons for giving back to the community might be, remember that even one of the greatest artistic minds of the previous century understood the importance of striving to make a difference. His intentions helped him to achieve the symbolic status, which is still present in many aspects of our culture. Have others in mind, give back, and provide a nurturing environment for the future generations. Don't forget: somebody did this for you in the past.

4. Conclusion

Life has a tendency to be complex and diverse. Every step we take, every decision we make gives us the opportunity to learn something new, something that can help us to better understand our place in this world.

Every life is something special and unique and as such priceless. However, there are lives that have the ability to change the world, its values and ideals. They are endowed with aptness to change the existing realities and shape new ones. As the time passes they are remembered, respected and serve as a norm which most strive to reach.

Walt Disney definitely belongs to this category. His charisma and aptitude change the course of history in the field of live animation and pushed the limits of entertainment to new, never before seen levels. Albeit his effect, that was only the beginning of his influence on the world we live in. He dared when no one else did, he hoped when there was no reason for hope and he marched on despite all the obstacles on his way. Much of his actions can serve us as teaching aids and a lot can be gained from them.

The importance of virtues such as self-esteem, confidence and courage appear first when analyzing the most important events of his life. Without them his journey to the world of animation would probably ended even before it actually started. Ingenuity propelled him further and allowed him to join the over-sea soldiers, where he started to develop a business sense which he only upgraded when he returned home. If failure was more than just a mental construct for him, he would probably soon abandon the thought of a career in animation. But he didn't. He overcame his emotional attachments and despite some negative experiences kept the drive to pursue his dreams. Endlessly he pushed the limits of existing schemes and with a clear understanding of his unique role and the ability to accommodate when it was necessary, he became an idol, a modern day legend and a mentor for new generations of young artists and businessmen.

Next time when you are trapped in creative block, remember that factors that can propel creative thinking and behavior can also be found in your environment, you just need to know where to look. When you open your mind and expect the unexpected without limiting your experience with predefined judgments, you have the opportunity to take the lessons learned from his actions and apply them to your situation.

Staying committed to yourself and embracing the opportunities that might occur when least expected, is still the most important part of creative behavior and thinking and will further develop your ability to think outside the box. This way, no problem will remain unsolved, and no solution will remain hidden from you.

BOOKS FROM MICHAEL WINICOTT

Another titles by Michael Winicott you may find interesting:

BILL GATES: BUSINESS LESSONS

BRAIN: EXERCISES TO EMPOWER

BUSINESS PLAN: A practical guide

FACEBOOK MARKETING: Business Lessons from Mark Zuckerberg

HABITS: MICRO CHANGES for MACRO RESULTS

HENRY FORD: ENTERPRENEURSHIP LESSONS

JESUS: LEADERSHIP LESSONS

LEONARDO DA VINCI: CREATIVITY LESSONS

MARTIN LUTHER KING: LIFE LESSONS

OPRAH WINFREY: LIFE LESSONS

STEVE JOBS: BUSINESS LESSONS

WINSTON CHURCHILL: LEADERSHIP LESSONS

DID YOU ENJOY THIS BOOK?

Thanks for purchasing and reading this book. If you reached this page you had probably enjoyed it. Would you care to leave a positive review in Amazon?

This is very important for 2 reasons:

a) I need your feedback to improve the quality of my books

b) Other people may read and benefit from this book if you share your thoughts.

 Thanks a lot!

Michael Winicott